Written by Dorine Barbey
Illustrated by Agnes Mathieu
and Sylvaine Perols

Specialist advisers:
Dr Sally Hope, Dr Anthony Hope
and Dr Jane Mainwaring

ISBN 1 85103 098 0
First published 1990 in the United Kingdom
by Moonlight Publishing Ltd,
36 Stratford Road, London W8
Translated by Sarah Matthews

© *1989 by Editions Gallimard*
English text © *1990 by Moonlight Publishing Ltd*
Typeset by Saxon Printing Ltd, Derby
Printed in Italy by La Editoriale Libraria

POCKET • WORLDS

The Five Senses

How do we get to know
the world around us?

We learn about the world through our senses. Thanks to them we can see beautiful landscapes, hear music, taste delicious cakes, smell the scent of flowers and feel the softness of their petals.

We have five senses: sight, hearing, smell, taste and touch. Your eyes, ears, nose, tongue and skin are the organs of your senses. They detect sensations and send messages to your brain. If it wants you to do something about the sensation – bite the apple, stroke the cat – your brain will send other messages to your muscles, through the nerves in charge of those movements.

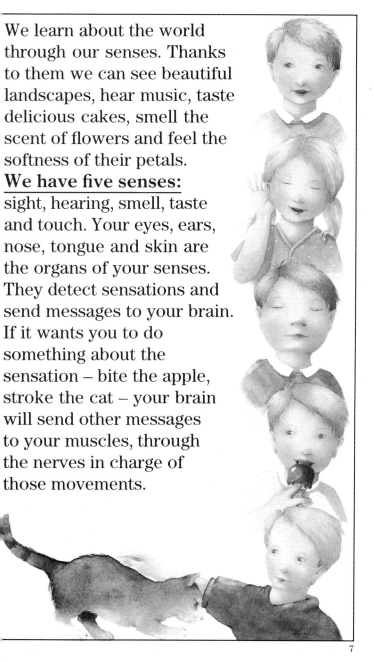

The eye is a soft globe protected by eyelids. It is set in a cavity called the orbit.

1. Cornea 2. Iris 3. Pupil 4. Lens 5. Retina 6. Optic nerve

Tears wash the eye constantly, keeping it moist. They are spread across the eyeball by the eyelids, which blink about once every ten seconds.

Sight carries all sorts of important information to the brain. The iris, which can be brown, blue, grey or green, is protected by the transparent cornea and has an opening in the middle, called the pupil. The lens behind the pupil changes shape according to whether the eye is looking at things close up or far away. Light passes through the pupil and falls on the retina at the back of the eye. Information is carried from the retina to the brain by the optic nerve.

Eyes can move a lot, quickly and in every direction, thanks to the muscles which fix them to the orbit.

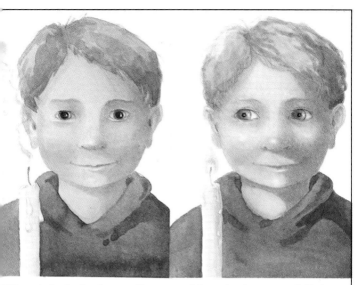

When it is dark, the pupil opens wide to let in as much light as possible. In bright light, though, it becomes very small.

Tears taste salty because they contain a chemical which stops bacteria from settling on the eye. They drain out of little channels, or ducts, in the corner of the eye. These ducts link up with the nose, which is why your nose drips when you cry!

As the lens focuses an image on the retina, it turns the picture upside down. When the brain receives the information, it turns the image the right way up again.

A horse cannot see clearly things which are directly ahead, but it can see a long way to either side.

We cannot see as far to the side as a horse can, but we do see more clearly, because the vision of each eye overlaps.

Eagles are very sharp-sighted, and can spot their prey, a mouse for instance, from a great height.

Insects' eyes are made up of thousands of tiny lenses. They see an image made up of dots, in colours quite different from the ones we see.

Insects see ultra-violet colours that we cannot see.

Dragon-flies have up to 40,000 tiny lenses in each eye. Their eyes cover almost the whole of their heads.

Nocturnal animals, which sleep by day and feed by night, have eyes that can see particularly well in the dark. An owl's eyes are a hundred times more sensitive to light than our eyes.

The little tarsier, a nocturnal animal related to the lemur, has the biggest eyes in proportion to its size of any mammal.

A chameleon can look in two directions at once, since its eyes swivel round independently of each other.

A short-sighted person sees distant things with a blurred outline. Glasses make the image clear.

Some people cannot see any difference between red and green, or sometimes blue. They are colour-blind.

Do you wear glasses?

If you do, it is because your eyes do not work perfectly. Short-sighted people cannot see clearly a long way off; long-sighted people have trouble seeing things close to. Glasses help to focus the image clearly on the retina.

Do these two shapes look the same to you? Trace over one of them and then lay the tracing over the other shape. Does it fit?

Can you believe your eyes?

Sometimes we cannot make sense of what we see. **Optical illusions** give us false information, so that our brain cannot interpret the image correctly.

Do the vertical lines look parallel to you?

Which of these figures is the taller? Use a ruler to check. Were you suprised?

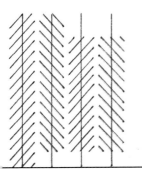

Outer ear
1. Auricle 2. Auditory canal

Middle ear
3. Tympanum (eardrum)
4. Ossicles (ear bones)

Inner ear
5. Semicircular canals
6. Cochlea

What do your ears do?

They send sounds to your brain, which works out where they come from and what they mean.

Sounds are vibrations which move through the air. Stretch an elastic band between your finger and thumb. If you twang it, you will see it vibrate and hear a tiny sound.

If you throw a pebble into the water, ripples move outwards from where it fell. In the same way, sound-waves move through the air.

Sound travels more quickly through the earth. Native Americans pressed their ears to the ground to listen for horsemen galloping towards them.

The tympanum vibrates like a drumskin. The louder the sound, the more the tympanum vibrates. Behind it lie three tiny bones, called the stirrup, the hammer and the anvil, because of their shapes. They transmit the vibrations to the cochlea, a curled tube full of liquid, which turns the vibrations into signals that are sent along the auditory nerve to the brain.

The semi-circular canals in your inner ear are your centre of balance. If you spin round for a while, then stop, you will find it hard to keep your balance. This is because the liquid in your ears is still moving, even though you are not!

Not all ears are the same.

Foxes and dogs can pick up a much wider range of sounds than we can. They can also prick up their ears and wiggle them to find out exactly where the sound is coming from. Birds have two tiny holes in the sides of their heads: these are their ear-openings. They have no outer ears.

The barn-owl can find a mouse in the blackest night. It has very sensitive hearing which helps it pick up even faint sounds.

Fish have special auditory organs on their skin which work like ears.

Crickets' ears are on their legs. Male crickets 'sing' by rubbing special veins on the bases of their wings. Each type of cricket has its own song.

Sounds underwater

We people do not hear much underwater, but that is not because it is silent down below. Some fish snore, others mutter or whistle; they are talking to each other. Cod sing to attract a mate!

Some moths have a special 'ear' which can register ultra-sounds too high-pitched for our ears. With this ear, the moth can hear the squeaks of any approaching bats.

Caterpillars are covered in hairs which react to noise. At the slightest sound, the caterpillars lie quite still, hoping that they won't be seen – and eaten.

What is a smell made of?

Countless tiny chemical particles float in the air which you breathe. Inside your nose are smell detectors called olfactory receptors, covered with tiny hairs. These receptors are bombarded with all sorts of different smells which they report to the brain. Then your brain has to sort out what they mean. A delicious smell of fresh baking wafting from the kitchen will make you feel hungry, thinking of freshly-cooked chocolate cake!

A newborn baby recognizes its mother's smell and is comforted by it. In the same way, a mother can recognize the scent of her own baby.

The scent linking mothers and babies is even more important among animals. Smell is often like an identity card. An ant colony will reject a strange ant passing by, because it does not smell right to them.

Peculiar noses!

The longest nose in the world is the elephant's trunk. It is very sensitive; elephants can sniff things out from over 1.5 kilometres away. Proboscis monkeys from Borneo have very big, bulgy noses, while the elephant seal's nose gets bigger with every year that passes, and doubles in size when the seal is angry!

Baby elephant

Proboscis monkey

Elephant seal

Moles are almost completely blind, but they have very sensitive noses to help them find their food in the dark. Star-faced moles, like this one, have feelers on the end of their noses as well.

The male silkworm moth has feathery antennae which are sensitive to tiny amounts of smell.

What are insects' antennae for?

Insects use them to smell with, as well as to help them find their way around. Bees use their antennae to taste the flowers.

Birds have very little sense of smell.

Their nostrils are usually to be found at the back of their beaks.

Fish have a very strong sense of smell.

It is smell which leads sharks to their prey. Rays, eels and catfish are very sensitive to smells. If a squid is attacked by a conger eel, it squirts out a black ink, momentarily blinding its attacker and blotting out its sense of smell.

A snake collects smell with its forked tongue which flickers in and out, picking up scents from the air and then taking the smell particles into the snake's mouth.

Tongues are sensitive to temperature and consistency as well as taste.

Children's taste-buds are much more sensitive than a grown-up's.

How do we taste things? We use our tongues. Look at your tongue: it is covered with taste-buds. Each one is sensitive to a particular kind of taste.

Our tongues are better at telling the difference between sweet and salt tastes than between bitter and acid ones. Even before it is born, a baby prefers sweet-tasting things. Fortunately, the growing child learns to enjoy other tastes as well.

The sense of taste is closely linked to the sense of smell. If you have a cold, it is difficult to tell what things taste like.

The four different kinds of taste: sweet (sugar), acid (lemon), bitter (chicory), salty (salt).

Every country has different traditions about what tastes good; some peoples like very spicy foods, others prefer sweet ones.

An exciting variety of different foods is enjoyed around the world. How many of these have you tasted?

If you gently touch a butterfly's foot with a paintbrush soaked in sugared water, the butterfly will unroll its long tongue.

The taste organs of insects such as bees, wasps and ants are found on their antennae.
Butterflies and flies have theirs in tiny hairs on the ends of their legs and on their feet. Watch how a fly treads on things to taste them before starting to eat.

When a wasp lands on a jam sandwich, it sweeps its antennae across quickly. It is smelling and tasting the sandwich at one and the same time.

Snails taste with
their antennae.

A parrot always tastes its food with its tongue
before eating it.

Fish like barbels and cat-fish use the
sensitive feelers all around their mouths to
explore underwater. They are touching
and tasting at the same time.
Octopi have taste-receptors all along their
tentacles.

Octopi also have very good eyesight to help them
catch their prey.

Our fingertips are very sensitive because we have a lot of nerve-endings there.

The sense of touch is located in the skin.

It is sensitive to the gentleness of a caress, the warmth of a kiss, the cold of an ice-cube, the sharp prick of an injection.

The scaly skin of a chicken's feet and the horny hooves of a deer or horse are not as sensitive as the skin of a snake.

Your whole body is covered with a thin layer of skin, which is full of sensitive nerve endings.
Skin reacts to touch, and will send messages to the brain to let you know how to react. So when somebody treads on your toes, it hurts and your brain tells you to get your foot out of the way!

Newborn babies are always trying to put things in their mouths. It is because that is where their skin is most sensitive. They can learn a lot about things in that way. A mother's caressing touch soothes her baby, and makes it calm and happy.

Different touch impressions:

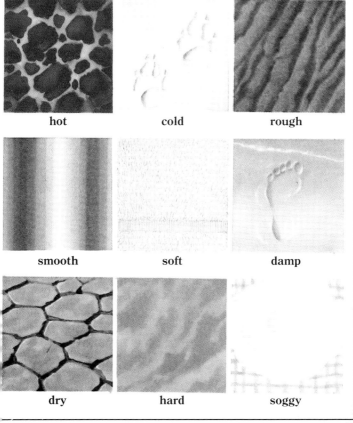

hot	**cold**	**rough**
smooth	**soft**	**damp**
dry	**hard**	**soggy**

During courtship, pelicans
touch each other a lot to
get to know
each other.

Penguins court in the same way.
But when they are heading back to their colonies,
they use their voices to find their
friends.

A baby kangaroo has hardly
any sense of smell
when it is born.

During its first six months,
spent in its mother's pouch, the
baby uses its sense of touch to find
her nipples under her thick fur.

What do they touch with?

Spiders spin and repair their webs constantly, using their hairy feet. The hairs are their organs of touch.

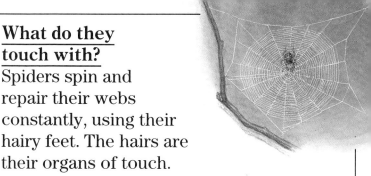

Amazonian ants hold feet to make a bridge over obstacles in their path.

Bees can tell the shape of things very accurately by using their antennae. A cat's whiskers help it to judge width and tell the cat whether it will fit through a gap.

The tiny shrew uses its whiskers to find its way around as well. This mother is showing her babies around their territory. They all hang on to each other so that they don't get lost.

Some animals have a special sense.

Something awful is going to happen. What can it be? The hens are panicking, the mice are trembling, the swallows are twittering. They know something the people don't know.

Animals are particularly sensitive to vibrations so that they can, for instance, judge when there is going to be an earthquake.

Before flies take wing, they stretch out their antennae to find out how hard the wind is blowing. Mosquitoes are very sensitive to temperature. Female mosquitoes, which feed on blood, can sense the presence of a warm-blooded animal or person from several metres away. They find you and bite you, even in the dark!

Using their sonar, dolphins can explore huge distances or locate another animal very precisely.

Dolphins have a sixth sense.

Like all cetaceans, dolphins and whales use sonar. They send out sounds which bounce off the objects around them. The nature and direction of the echo tell them the shape of the object and how far away it is.

The ray sends out electrical charges which paralyse its prey or frighten off its attackers.

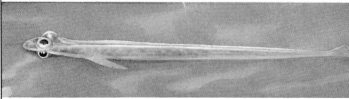

The four-eyed fish, or anableps, can see underwater and above the surface at the same time.

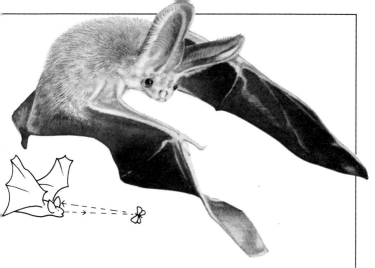

Bats have sonar too.

Their ultra-sonic squeaks are too high-pitched for us to hear. The bats' sensitive ears pick up the echoes, which guide them as they fly and help them hunt their prey.

How do migrating birds find their way around?

Like homing pigeons, they navigate by the position of the sun by day, and the stars by night. This is called 'astronomical navigation'.

The stuff of memory!

Catch a whiff of the smell of a pine wood
or the murmur of waves on the sea-shore...
and it conjures up your summer holidays
so clearly! Your senses trigger
your brain and bring back
all the memories associated
with a particular experience.

Exercise your senses.

For instance, chew your bread for as long
as possible before you swallow it, and
discover how the bread slowly changes
taste and texture.

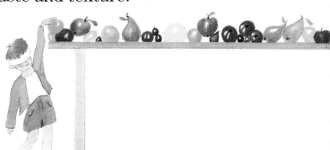

**Blindfold yourself, and see if
you can recognize different fruits
by the way they feel and smell.**

People do not all experience things with exactly the same intensity. Some have one sense or another particularly well developed. For instance, some people have what is called absolute pitch. They can tell the difference between every musical note they hear.

People who invent perfumes have a particularly well developed sense of smell, which can detect the subtlest differences between scents.

If you do not pay attention to your senses, you may find yourself living in a dull, muffled kind of way. But if you concentrate on what they tell you, you will find that your body opens out on to a world of wonderful variety full of colours, scents, tastes, sounds . . . Your senses will help you get the very best out of life! If you have lost, or were born without one of your senses, you probably have developed the others far more than your friends who have all of theirs.

Index

Pocket Worlds – building up into a child's first encyclopaedia: